Role Reversal

Turn Pain Into Power

Role Reversal

Turn Pain into Power

Candie Ferald

Little Girl Productions, LLC. Richmond, Va

Role Reversal: Turn Pain Into Power

Final Edition

To Cathy;
Best wishes in all
your heart's desires.
Stay sweet; be blessed.
♥ Candie

Dedicated
to the
Discouraged

♥

Inspired
by the
Daring

In memory of
my beloved
Papa

♥

Thanks for everything.

Table of Contents

Chapter 1

Soul For Hostage

1- Soul For Hostage

I held my soul for hostage,
   thinking I could extort from the Lord
   and that move that I made,
   is one I could never afford
   and though He saved me anyway,
   I dare do that no more.

I put up for ransom,
   this me
   that I thought I owned
   but He made me quickly to realize
   my life from Him is a loan.

I tried to call it quits,
   throw in my earthly towel.
I became self destructive,
   leaving my soul to be devoured.

Definitely I had had it,

I had given up on this life.
I was angry with the Lord,
  access to my soul,
  I tried to deny.

He knew what I was feeling,
  that I felt so torn apart.
He had planned already my deliverance.
It was prepared before life's start.

I'm not boasting nor am I bragging
  how I turned away from God...
  just shouting He brought me back...
  so changed,
  but just as loved.

The road isn't always easy.
At times, it is bitter, cold and hard
  but faith is a must have
  whether traveling a mile, an inch or a yard.

Bridges were definitely burned.
Curses fervently spoken

but never did my sweet Lord Jesus,
    never did He stop His working.

It's tragic how much time I wasted
    trying to fight with God.
How was I to beat Him?
He gave me these two arms.

2– The Deciding Factor

Away must go my vice.
On this day do I decide–
  no longer its causes and effects
  am I able to easily hide.

I must pull out
  some of these skeletons
  from inside
  my crowded closet.

I need feature only myself
  as my most capable runaway partner.

I ran from my demons,
  they were most gruesome and dark.
I planned to run all my life
  but finally I was caught.

Owning yourself isn't always easy.

It can be a gut wrenching task,
   but the realities of my own anecdotes
   placed my dreams under attack.

Don't know how I am going to do it...
   for today is only day one
   but I know nothing will compare
   to the feeling when I'm done.

Don't know how it will happen
   but I know it will occur.
It's no longer up for debate.
I've given my soul my word.

I'm putting this thing aside
   called my foolish pride,
   learning when I flee from myself,
   my destiny also hides.

I've fled in the bottle,
   fleeing from my anger.
I've fled in the woota,
   to make my heart a stranger.

I've fled in the plate
   to over 300 pounds.
I've fled with a bitter tongue,
   assaulting with nasty rounds.

It's been on my mind
   for quite some time
   this sabotage of my own pursuits.
I wasn't just enjoying these things,
   they were downright and often abused.

I can't catch hold of my blessings
   if my soul is caught and bound.
Why surrender to the past
   when my best is yet to be found?

So I've decided most absolutely
   certain patterns must become obsolete.
Actions must speak louder than words
   if my dreams and reality are to meet.

It may be only day one

but at least it's a beginning.
Gotta take that first step sometime
to reach my desired ending.

3– Temper

My temper is a beast
  I wish I could ignore.
Controlling and consoling it
  is often a burdensome chore.

It overwhelms me.
It scolds me,
  binds me to my past
  with it's stubborn and cold embrace.

It relentlessly rejects
  promising possibilities,
  leaving me unfeeling…

Where did it come from?

There are plenty of answers
  that explain everything
  yet they mean nothing at all.

Sometimes that unfeeling feeling
  is a welcome wall.
In reality sadly,
  it compromises so much joy.

Doesn't make sense to have all this good
  that's matched with likewise fury.
Doesn't feel right to explode
  and hurt those unaware and near me.

How can I contain this temper…
  to finally lay it to rest?
The answer remains elusive,
  perhaps this is my test.

A life more peaceful I pray for.
I hope He answers me soon.
He has much in store for me
  but my anger leaves little room.

4– The Exception

Jesus goes with everything.

From what you know
  to what you think,
From the middle of it all
  to the edge and the brink,
From the shutters and its windows
  to the kitchen and its sink.

And everything in between.

From the enormous
  to the minute,
From the huge
  to the petty
Need Jesus in your heart?
He's waiting there already,

Even when you run from Him

fearing the call of His lessons,
He remains in your heart
to guide you to your blessings.
Even in your darkest hour
when you're hated by them all.
Even when you've brought on your troubles
and there is no one left to call.

Even when I hid in the rocks
and other forms of self destruction,
never did He love me less,
there was no such deduction.
I've testified many times
of the numerous facts and details.
The only way I escaped myself
is because God's love prevails.

Jesus didn't scatter when
I tried to push Him aside.
He kept loving me anyway,
nourishing the seeds He planted inside.

He was there in those times

my eyes couldn't see.
He'll be there in the end
  when my lungs no longer breathe.
I know He's even here
  in these words that I've poured,
  especially in those words
  I don't want to own anymore.

I pushed Him away
  yet and still He came.
How could I ever hesitate
  to call on His perfect name?

In all those places
  I knew for certain
  He couldn't possibly be,
  He existed all the same
  just to rescue me.

I don't believe in Jesus
  because of what the others say.
It's just the one thing
  He wouldn't do for me–
  is He wouldn't go away.

5– The Turning Tide

I was in the turning tide,
  my travels hard to conceive,
  such a miraculous return from the dark,
  some details you'd never believe…

Once my heart and mind were made up
  to free myself from the rock,
  I had to devise a plan
  so it's control over me would stop.

I couldn't make it cold turkey,
  rehab way out of the question.
I would have to do it by weening,
  my soul's top suggestion.

I knew it wouldn't be easy,
  my insides it had taken hold
  so I had to slip away quietly,
  silently, to reclaim my soul.

I once smoked up to four wootas a night
   then eased the number to three-
   quietly and silently,
   to let the light back into me.

With my spirit now reawakened,
   I knew I could make it to two...
   so I challenged myself even further
   to see what my will could do.

With freedom on the horizon,
   my goal was to level it to one.
Slowly but surely I secured that.
Still, my positioning wasn't done.

I had wrestled it down to one a day.
I started adding days in between,
   days became weeks, weeks became months-
   God, the head of this team.

Such a miraculous miracle
   obtained by baby small steps.

Now I'm here and I can't count the years
  since Satan's weapon has been cast.

My enemy's tool was way stronger,
  had more pull than did I anticipate.
It took more than I knew I had
  to navigate my tricky escape.

Not only am I no longer captive
  but I had to fight my way to be free.
The devil's plans turned on their side
  and made a stronger soldier of me.

Nearly broken into pieces,
  a ship with many leaks.
The battle served this purpose–
  I am a vessel now uneasily breached.

6- Somebody's Missing

Have you ever missed somebody...
  missed somebody so much,
  it seems you could slip and die
  from the absence of their touch?
At times you'd like to crawl
  into their lowered grave
  just to hold them one more time,
  this beloved you could not save.

Have you ever missed somebody...
  missed somebody so hard,
  that you called into question
  the intentions of our Mighty God.
You demand He reveal the cause,
  why you must suffer because of love
  and how could this possibly bring you closer
  to trusting Him and His laws?

Have you ever missed somebody...

missed them so deep inside,
that you could easily drown
in the waves of tears you cried
and you wouldn't even notice
if the end itself were near-
had to be a mistake anyway
for them to be there and you here.

Have you ever missed somebody so much...
that it left you emotionally twisted,
that sometimes the memories seem a burden
instead of treasures forever gifted.

Most days the emotions you can muster
range from angry, bitter and confused
and nothing seems to comfort you,
not even the greatest or most desired of news.

It seems no reason to hurt anymore
cause that won't bring them back.
Doesn't matter how hard you fight-
the haunting sadness relentlessly attacks.
Have you ever missed somebody so deeply...

that it nearly dismantled your heart?
That only learning to let go of them
 allowed the healing to start.

7- About Face

I think sometimes she doesn't love me
   cause I look like my "dad"
   and the way that he treated her
   left her angry, scared and sad.

He was such a smooth talker that
   she made many bad decisions.
She wasn't prepared to deal with
   the reality of their consequences.

He left her with a hole in her soul
   and two little girls to raise,
   overwhelming financial debt
   and a heart full of pain.

I can see it in her eyes sometimes,
   how she looks upon my face.
I'm a lifelong reminder
   of her mistakes and disgrace.

She doesn't bite her tongue.
Her hatred for him is clear.
I wonder if life would be better for her,
  if I were never here.

I know that she loves me
  though she rarely says the words.
I know she didn't mean to–
  to pass on so much hurt.

I won't have cosmetic surgery,
  no facial transformation or change.
I just wonder if all of my life
  from her, I will be estranged?

There are a few other reasons
  that we treat each other wrong
  but this is the only one
  that will last my whole life long.

8– Forbidden Love

I'm used to being so strong
  with an extra weight to bare
  and I'm used to doing it alone
  with no one willing to share.

They probably couldn't if they wanted,
  help me carry my load.
I could do all the carrying
  if the encouragement was a little bit more.

But how can you support
  what you can't understand?
That's why it's hard for me to trust
  any living woman or man.

Maybe I've been through too much
  to have an open heart.
Maybe my chance has ended
  before I knew it started.

There seems nowhere new to go
  that I haven't chanced before.
I fear using my emotional means
  to open uncertain doors.

I know what I need in my life,
  the human source appears hidden...
  which leads me to question
  is unconditional love,
  for some, forbidden?

And if it happens to be forbidden,
  is there something I can do...
  something to unlock the door
  to experience something new?

To many, commitment seems natural.
Freedom has best suited my needs.
If I pass on the notion of love,
  does it mean I'm giving up on me?

9– Smooth Move

We made love that very morning.
He kissed me as I dropped him off at work.
He said he'd see me later.
I had a plan to conquer the world.

I made that day a busy one.
Got part time work, cleaning tools and a loan.
I thought we were in agreement.
We were to build something of our own.

But quickly the tables turned
  and the respect I thought I'd earned,
  was lessened to absolutely nothing
  because his hateful words did I spurn.

He was using his words to hurt me,
  thought he knew how to make me cry.
He said he'd been holding something back,
  still don't know if it were true or a lie.

I shrugged off what he said,
   demanding I react in anger.
Never did such a smooth move
   result in such life threatening danger…

From the dining area to the kitchen,
   bounced liked a ball down the hall,
   all the way to the bathroom
   where the sink broke my fall
   and once again to the living room
   where my back was framed in the wall.
His choking hands then gained my breath
   until the Lord heard my muted call!

Narrowly, did I escape him…
   I could feel a part of me moving on
   but obviously I was meant to live,
   not meet death in this domestic storm.

That was almost ten years ago.
This is the first real thing
   about that day I've written.
Yes, it took me all that long

just to remove the sting of being bitten.

10– The Resulting Anger

I'll be the last one standing
   and on that you can bet.
You haven't seen a soul like me,
   a soul as determined yet.

I'll be the one to get you.
I'll deliver the critical blow.
You'll be asking me for mercy,
   begging, but I won't let go.

You'll be dazed, asking questions...
   where did she come from?
Then you catch my pretty eyes,
   can't you tell that I'm the one?

I'll be the one who'll crush you
   and rip you into shreds.
It's my goal to leave you wishing
   for a quick and timely death.

Didn't you hear my warning?
I'm sure I let you know,
  that if you challenge me,
  I'm aiming way pass the lowest blow.

Are you blind and can't you see
  that when I'm full of anger,
  I've questioned God in me?

Yet you continue to press it
  to push me into this game.
Can't you see there's something in me
  that won't answer to anyone's shame?
You'll cringe at the sound of my name.

You have no chance to defeat me,
  no chance to win this war.
Because if I have to do it,
  I'll certainly do it all.

Taking my kindness for weakness
  has proven your fatal flaw.

Why summon that part of me–
  that part willing to ignore God.

I'll do what you'd never think of,
  some move that will take your breath.
Are you now understanding...
  you haven't truly seen me yet?

What more is there?
You foolishly dare
  questioning me and my game…
You'll never forget,
  I'll be sure to inflict
  some mind blowing pain.

My ultimate goal is to win this war–
  some things I know I must lose.
If you want to pay the cost of trying me,
  my actions will most fervently prove...

The only true fear I claim
  is fear of the wrath of God
  and the only way to serve Him

is to make sure that I survive.

Chapter 2

♥

Sordid and Sorted

1– Sordid and Sorted

My biological
  knocked on my door
  just the other day.

I didn't even open it
  to turn him away.

He was just standing there
  wondering if we were at home
  but my soul's protection
  required I leave him alone.

We called up our mother
  to seek her advice.
Told my sister answer the door.
Be at least that nice.

He asked her for three dollars.
I had plenty more.

I could count that in the change
  that was thrown about my floor.

I bet he knew I was watching
  but myself I wouldn't show.
He left without that three dollars.
I couldn't wait for him to go.

You might think that's quite nasty
  but I really don't give a damn.
It took me 33 hard years
  to sort him from who I am.

2- The Anti-Pain Pursuit

What thoughts do you claim...
 when you hear the word pain
 and you allow your thoughts to flow?

Do you know?
Are you scared?
Have you ever faced your demons before?

Many self truths you should explore.

Pain, uncontrollable suffering is
 what we flee from the most
 and it's usually because
 we can't pinpoint its source.

So, what thoughts do you claim...
 when I say the word pain
 and you no longer fear what you see?
As the puzzle begins to unfold,

you recall the unsatisfied need.

Do you feel alone?
Do you feel ashamed?
Can you even dig deep enough
    to uncover its awful name?

Whatever the monkey,
    whatever the thorn,
    whatever we suffer,
    whatever we endure...
We do so for a reason
    and you must face it with full stead,
Think you can deny sadness, silly human?
Only living life can defeat death.

Pain is just an inevitable thing,
    yet there is one method I faithfully employ...
    the best defense is a good offense.
Defeating my demons leaves room for joy.

3- Children of the Pipe

When a parent first smokes rock,
  it is a choice that was made.
It is an option that addiction
  quickly snatches away.

This choice affects their love,
  how they are able
  to give or receive.
It influences each and every piece
  of their baby's basic needs,
  weighing down heavily
  on their child's hopes and dreams,
  if...

IF they ever even develop any.

Parental addiction has soul changing effects.
This child becomes fearful of what's coming next.
It plagues the growth of reasoning,

how to define the worst from the best.
It promotes it as normal,
   the constant struggle for less.

Sometimes these children
   build unhealthy walls,
   needed to protect their heart
   from rock's far reaching claws,
   and the rock, it is insatiable.
It wants everything.

Competing with the rock
   for love and attention,
   these children adapt
   to losing not winning.
In a constant state of suspicion
   of others' intentions,
   these children see things
   they dare never mention.

Rock pushes
   the worst of the past
   over the legacy of the future.

The myth of unconditional love
  seems cruel and elusive.

Many times curious kids
  follow those laid open tracks,
  wondering what this drug has
  that they obviously lack.
Sometimes they just hope
  to bring that lost parent back
  but mercy is never granted
  by Satan's soldier crack.

Children of the pipe,
  they do survive.
I've seen so for myself
  with my very own eyes.

What I still and
  have yet to surmise
  is why should a child
  have to pay such a price?

4– Further or Farther

I only wanted be happy,
  yet I've the rage of a beast.
I want to destroy my enemies
  using all the hate thriving in me.

How can my soul contain so much hate
  when it's filled with so much love?
How can I live in peace
  feeling so torn apart?

How can I become this angry
  when God resides in my soul?
My emotions are easily justified
  yet I worry over their control.

What a scared existence I behold,
  trying to follow the Lord.
God created and sustains me
  yet the devil beckons and entertains me.

What a creature,
  this child that I am–
  that when my Father calls,
  I sometimes hide further within.

My actions reflect
  what needs I put first
  and as written,
  I'm dying of thirst.

How shall I travel in response to this plight...
  furthermore into the darkness
  or Father, more into the light?

By circumstance, I am furious,
  ready to strike a deafening blow–
  yet I've learned to wait and listen
  for instruction from the Lord.

Knowing all the while,
  God still recognizes the light,
  the one He planted in my heart

to overcome the darkness
that swallows me when I doubt.

There is a path indeed,
  a straight and narrow way
I pray I have what's required
  to walk it well some day.

5- 6ooooh9

It is a thought that makes itself present
  each and everyday.
It is an inhabitant of my head
  that will not go away...
  a remembrance of a dream
  recurring nearly 25 years.
I can hardly sleep now
  in fear it will reappear.

It was like a roller coaster ride
  but there was no amusement.
I was trapped in a big, white car
  furiously and mysteriously moving,
  rocketing out of control
  down a dark and winding road.
All the windows were down,
  the night air punishing and cold.

The wind whipped against my skin

and I was screaming all the while.
The car wouldn't stop
  containing this terrified child.

Sometimes childhood characters
  appeared in the driver's seat.
In this dream they were predators
  and I, a delicious treat.

The vicious woodpecker wasn't playing–
  it had shining, razor sharp teeth,
  so did that menacing werewolf
  and it was my heart he was going to eat.
Clowns were usually funny
  but wicked and sinister this one's laugh.
The hulk was my all time favorite
  but an evil villain, his part in this cast.

Then sometimes the driver's seat would be empty.
There would be no one driving at all
  but never did that stop
  the course of this rocketing car.

What made me have this dream,
  the same things over and over again?
What could have possibly happened that night
  to cause this nightmare to begin?

I called up and asked my mom,
  explaining the thoughts wouldn't go away.
She was shocked and saddened to hear
  I had any traces of that day.
It wasn't just a dream she said,
  that night happened for real...
  wasn't no make believe character
  but a person manning the wheel.

It wasn't just some car ride.
He wasn't trying to thrill us–
  that night he was having a breakdown.
He was trying to kill us.

Somehow, in her telling me
  of that night on 609,
  there came some relief to me.
It was no deficit of my mind.

I haven't had that nightmare in awhile.
It has since in my dreams failed to creep
  but how can I ever really know for sure
  when I still struggle so to sleep.

6– Endurance

I dare not confess
　the anger I feel sometimes
　thinking on the heavy hits
　I've taken in life–

The bitter irony of knowing
　that for far too long,
　pain has pressed me forward.
　What an excellent motivation
　pain has been.

How many struggles can I count?
A startling amount,
　in all shapes and forms,
　some devastating storms.

Sometimes in the midst of these storms,
　I feel that who I am
　is not enough

and I search for worldly security
in the very things
set before me
as tools for my destruction.

Yet God's grace and mercy
  have grounded me to this path.
He has granted me strength
  so my stride will last.

He has granted me guidance
  and centered my heart.
Deliverance was assured
  before my life's start.

God has done everything for me.
I won't turn back now.
To His awesome and absolute power,
  my soul humbly bows.

Whatever goodness I have
  is the result of God.
My faith will grow

despite what comes.

Though the road can be treacherous
  and I've often stumbled.
With the love of God,
  I shall endure the struggle.

7- My Favorite

I only fit well
  between these two pages,
  gliding across time
  engaging my various faces.
The ones that work
  versus those that won't–
  the me's that are the problem
  are at times, the anecdote.

What could poison the air
  sweetens my paper.
Experience has taught me well
  to avoid unfulfilling capers
  and to retreat from foolish things
  before I become entangled and caught–
  to learn successful strategies
  from the battles I have fought.

Peace for much too long

had been the prize of my fight.
A soul without peace
  is a gut wrenching sight
  and since the spirit of truth
  has wrapped itself in my soul,
  nothing will satisfy me
  until my story's been told.

My eyes remained on this prize,
  evolution created its difference.
The spirit of truth communed with my soul
  to form an everlasting commitment.

Is this love or a distraction?
Whichever way each life goes down–
  there are wars that must be fought
  and we all must choose our ground.

Paper is my favorite.

8– Regret, None

Regret during troubling times
  does no one good
  except the devil.

Punishing self doubt
  figures prominently
  on all new decisions.

Can't think with a heavy mind.

You're at your best
  when you leave
  the mistake behind.

Just take the lesson with you.

You may have been warned,
  maybe severely scorned.

You may have been bad,
  would retract what you said.

You may have seen it coming
  but couldn't react
  to the warning.

There may have been,
  could have been
  many things
  that went down different.

Can't question it now
  because you know
  deep down inside...

  .

You made your choices for a reason.

9– Traveling

I've done so much
  under the sun
  that was contrary to my upbringing.
Living with the shame
  heavily distorted my thinking.

I became a prisoner to my skeletons,
  fearing their exposure.
I shied away from my path,
  thinking my chances were over.

I erected walls of protection
  so I could complete my journey
  but the walls nearly collapsed on me.
All those chips became a burden.

There's still a lot of road ahead.
I must clear my guilty vision.
I choose to take God at His Word

and confess to receive forgiveness.

I hold myself accountable for any devastation,
I've participated fully
   in my soul's degradation.

To my merciful God,
   these things I here now confess–
Confident of His forgiveness,
   my past is laid to rest.

I lied and I cheated,
   envied and stole,
   been with plenty who were unworthy,
   basically living like a whore.

I talked down to some who didn't deserve it,
Argued often with my mother.
I laced my weed with rock
   to rebel over losing my brother.

I fought with my younger brother,
   did the same with my sister thrice,

Threatened my father while I was high
  and told him I'd take his life.

In a rage, I destroyed a few things,
  abandoned more than one friend,
  used my tongue as a weapon...
  and begged for this pain to end.

Why would I admit these things...
  to elicit ridicule for my errors?
I won't be by my past,
  held over anyone's barrel.

Why would I admit these things...
  knowing how true they are?
I had to let go of that baggage.
I plan on getting far.

Why would I not admit these things...
  to testify how He changed me?
Despite all my transgressions,
  He still loves me enough to save me.

10- The Nothingness

Giving up is incompatible with my faith.
I'd easily reject the notion of its existence except
  I see folks doing so all around me
  seems all the time.
I become confused.

Giving up is so beneath my realm of thinking,
  I had to look up the words to even write this piece.
When I did so, my stomach became full of disgust.
  I imagined burning my dictionary except that I need and
  love it so,

Giving up is poles apart from anywhere I fancy myself.
It is absurd to a spiritually ambitious child of God
  who knows that He has plans for her,
Those plans were laid out and perfected
  even before the earth was warm.
All I have to do is show up and obey.

Allowing the option of giving up
   creates discord in my universe.
It has no place.
It is a spot of nothingness
   surrounded by an abundance of blessings
   the Lord is waiting to bestow upon me.
That spot must be obliterated.

Giving up doesn't apply to situations that are unnatural or
   wrong in the first place.
It does not apply to those things that are against God's will,
   those very things that our endurance and abilities are meant
   to change.

It is not the same as rearranging, resting, reevaluating,
   reconstructing or reconstituting.
It is unlike formulating a new route when the path is
   blocked.
It is unlike designing a new key when there is no other door
   to that particular goal.
It is not abandoning a mission that would otherwise lead you
   away from God's designs.
Giving up? It is bullshit and is different from anything I ever

want to know.

Chapter 3

♥

The Recount

1– As Long As I Live

As long as I live,
  one thought will not escape me,
I'll never be worthy
  of the way God blesses me.

During those times
  when I doubt the most and
  I sink in despair thinking all is lost,
  God is the one I am first to blame...
  why don't you help me...
  as I call on His name.

Where are You God,
  through these current struggles?
Why do you allow me to
  continuously suffer?

You are God and You hold all the power.
Where are You in my neediest of hours?

I need You Lord, I need you right now.
I need You to save me, save me somehow.

Do you hear me Lord as I beg of Your name?
Am I somehow caught in a religious game?
Am I a pawn in some spiritual war...
  to once feel God's love and then no more,
  to feel warm with blessings, then suddenly cold,
  wondering what I've done to be left all alone.

These are the thoughts that I allow to consume me
  when I'm deep in depression and my worries are many...
  then suddenly again, the Lord comes to save me,
  then suddenly again, the Lord comes to save me.

These are the words I have proclaimed repeatedly
  because of the ways the Lord has blessed me.
In my times of fear and faithless blasphemy,
  thank You Lord for carrying me through
  and for granting me mercy when I doubted You.

Who am I to doubt
  or even question Your Will?

Who am I Lord...
  but Your child still.

Thank You Lord,
  time and time again
  for holding me tight
  and letting me back
  into the fold again
  after I've wandered.

I'll never be worthy of You, my heavenly Father,
  and this is the one thing
  I'll know as long as I live.

2- Soul Ownership

I will not be quiet.
I will not tuck in my tail.
I will not be shamed to silence.
I will not be afraid to yell.

I will not let my social status
  restrain the truth of my lips.
I will stand up for myself
  even when my fear resists.

I will not let my bad experience
  taint how I feel about others.
I will not let you stand as innocent
  while I rattle, run and take cover.

I will own my emotions,
  they must be expressed.
Locking them in the inside
  only causes my soul duress.

I have a fiery spirit.
My sentiments run from beginning to end.
Sometimes they become my enemy.
Most times, they remain my friend.

They run intensely the full gamut.
They frequent many channels.
I will not let any living being
  convince me they don't matter.

That does not give me free reign
  to spew them all about.
It gives me the responsibility
  to at least speak when I should shout.

Owning how you feel inside
  is only how you begin.
Deal truthfully with your discoveries
  to position yourself to win.

3- Watch Me Die

Is death the creature
  that overtakes my body?
Or is death the disease
  that flows through my veins?

Is death the deterioration
  of my beautiful mind?
Or is death the captivity
  of my proud people?

Is death the shame
  of the complexion of my skin?
Or is death the needle
  that spits poison inside me?

Is death the snow
  that covers me
  in a euphoric blizzard?
Or is death the hatred

that sets my soul afire?

Is Death the confusion
  of not knowing where to turn...
  when it is justice and equality,
  for which all people yearn?

Or is death the darkness
  that took your soul away
  that you would deny
  any human being
  the simple human basics?

4– The Rock Mile

I know you on that shit again.
The evidence is abound.
You claim you so busy
  but progress is hardly found.

I ain't really seen you sober,
  been a minute since you been steady.
Even though you never have money,
  to go, you always seem ready.

I know the warning signs.
I got firsthand information.
I sat down at that table.
I indulged on that invitation.

At one time we both agreed
  that the hope on which we were feeding,
  was the very same device
  that stopped our wounds from healing.

Our ability and will to survive
  was severely compromised.
Satan poses as that rock,
  such a wicked and clever disguise.

The enemy knows your pressure points,
  life's blows that make you weak.
It knows where you lack coping skills
  and the help that you may seek.

Yes, the enemy is in the rock pile.
It wants you to know it's always an option.
Delighted to be your go-to guy,
  a forget all about it concoction.

It seems like fun and games at first
  but rock is called work for a reason.
With all you go through to score,
  only the high is easy.

If that rock seems like your friend,
  then you must be addicted.
The first step to freedom

is to have the balls to admit it.

Don't worry about what others say.
This just isn't about their life.
You don't have the time for them.
You'll need your strength for the fight.

The battle will take nearly all you have
  just to turn away from the pile
  and what ever little bit remains,
  you'll need to hike that mile.

5- The Dying Reply

With a graven sigh,
  Aunt Sweetie asked how I'd reply
  if I returned to my Maker
  "with all those drugs inside".

If the day I get to heaven,
  I was out of my mind high
  and what could I possibly say to Jesus
  if the drugs were why I died.

I was angry and bitter then,
  that was reflected in my answer.
Does it matter how I get there
  as long as I reach my master?

So I replied to my Auntie Sweetie...

Should I die in a car accident
  the same as took my brother?

Or be claimed by two bullets
  like my long time young lover?

Should I succumb to some awful disease
  that's conquered my flowing veins?
Maybe we'd understand each other
  if I shared more of my mother's pain…

But those words that I said,
  had been fed by rage
  which has now been softened
  by experience and age.

Since that talk with my Auntie,
  even more have passed on
  like that sweet key to my heart,
  that water sign now beyond..

In dealing with his death,
  former feelings did I revisit.
With the change in my ways,
  the dying reply is a bit different.

If Auntie were to ask again,
  I'd want it reflected in my answer
  that I overcame my many demons
  with the help of my merciful Master.

Though life's journey was sometimes rocky
  and at times, simply ill fated,
  that I'll return as God intended
  and He will recognize what He created.

Though God's Word won't return void,
  I am not relieved of my part.
I want my life to show my deep gratitude
  that his grace restored my heart.

My bitter response has long faded,
  like the habit with which it came.
The more room I make for Jesus,
  the less for the dark to remain.

6- Role Reversal

Pain into power my hurt will turn...
  a spiritual lesson is to be learned
  that obstacles increase my yearn
  while being underestimated makes me burn.
Sorrow's advance I constantly spurn.
My faith holds me steady and firm.
Pain into power, my will shall turn.

Power will come from my pain...
  no more ground will my enemy gain
  by my intent not being made plain.
My way to the kingdom I wish to gain
  and I can't do that by remaining the same
  so I call unto Jesus' name...
What we gonna do with this pain?

Pain power let us make it into...
  don't forget that life is time God lends you,
  that's why the enemy wants to win you

so far apart from God he can send you.
His purpose is to do more than just bend you.
He wants for himself the gifts God gives you.
What better than power to make pain into?

Turn your pain into power...
  manage its caustic showers.
Under its duress dare not you cower,
  for you know who's waiting to devour
  souls that by suffering have been soured.
Your faith is an invincible tower–
  from that source, build your power.

7– The Family's Business

For some, legitimacy is not even a target,
  hardly a fair shot growing up on the block.
Uneven is the playing field
  when you're socialized by the rock.

It's more than uneven.
It's faulty to the core.
Surrounded by such an evil,
  it's hard to envision more.

It's difficult to dream
  when surrounded by sadness.
It's suppresses education
  when home life is madness.

It promotes distrust
  to see the worst of people.
It's natural to become numb
  protecting yourself from evil.

Limited seem life's options
  when scrutinized by poisoned voices.
Most people learn by what they experience.
The family's business injects its choices.

These babies learn the whole system
  from the buy, the processing, the sale.
All facets of the trade become normal
  even the consequences of jail.

Some youngsters go to Disney World
  or are sent off to camp each summer.
Some get trust funds on their birthdays,
  their future's promise is never a wonder.

Some will never know pangs of hunger
  or see a bare Christmas tree.
Their childhood is true freedom,
  'cause they have everything they need.

I'd never want this pain for others,
  just want everyone to understand,

it's hard to play the game
when dealt a shaky hand.

Imagine were this your child's everyday life
   and all that they usually saw?
What kind of start would that be
   and how could they shoot for the stars?

Society brands them as monsters,
   trying to keep their families fed.
Where do the street dealers get their drugs?
Shouldn't we be asking that instead?

So why does the rock exist,
   if it tears families and communities apart?
So some rich lady can have her furs
   and some rich man have his yacht?

Who all is making all the big money?
It's not the young boys on the yard.
Who all is making all the real money?
It's not the young girls on the yard.
Follow the path to the big dollars

and we'll see who the gangsters are.

Being the good person that you strive to be,
  you ask what effect can you really have.
One that is loud and far reaching-
  the direction money and ballots are cast.

The business of the family-
  what just happens to flow down the line
  will at least be the first point of reference
  for how our lives are defined.

We all have to make a choice
  on how to carry on our family's business.
Just don't be surprised that some
  have more complicated decisions.

8– Brainiac *(sexual content)*

I want you to make love to me
  starting with my brain,
  then the lovemaking will be so beautiful,
  we'll do it over and over again.

The motions would be over
  only because we came,
  our bodies mixing so deliciously,
  producing sweat and semen rains.

Even the act of just talking to you
  leaves me light and lifted.
If all the Lord did
  was just invent you,
  He'd still be entirely as gifted.

I'm thinking about you
  right here and now,
  like I've been all day,

wondering if I've been in your thoughts
in some sizzling and sexy way.

My body oozes with desire
  because you intoxicate my mind.
A sexual adventure could await us,
  a spectacularly climactic time.

Your flirtations leave me warm and fuzzy,
  sometimes even smoking hot.
They've given me extreme confidence
  of your abilities to soothe my spot.

If we ever exchange orgasms,
  let us wait til we can't wait no more,
until we're both so ripe and ready,
  we break the bed down to the floor.

Lovemaking may be on the horizon
  and if yes be my final decision,
  just as you do for my mind,
  make my body your mission.

9– A Little Thing Called Faith

Let the spirit rock me.
Let it command my name.
When the motion is over,
  let only the good remain.

Let its love consume me,
  gently swaying my soul.
For surely does its' awesome power,
  demand I surrender control.

Let my light shine brightly,
  if only for a moment.
When the blame is mine,
  smarten me to own it.

Let me not be weary,
  the hymn sweetly plays.
Let not my pride again
  separate me and His way.

Allow my heart to mend,
  beginning with forgiveness.
Let me fear nothing
  but God's claim to vengeance.

Let my journey be meaningful,
  a testimony that He is.
Open my mind to treasure
  the magnitude that exists.

Teach me to walk the path dear Jesus
  despite my weakness and fear
  and never let me forget...
It started with a little faith,
  the thing that got me here.

10- The Recount

You may not be taking score
  but I'm adding up all the facts.
You've designated for yourself a hero
  the very enemy holding you back..

You rationalize so much why you need it-
  without it you can't survive.
It's the only reason you wake sometimes.
It makes it worth the staying alive.

It pushes you to keep going-
  makes this rough life soft.
It's the only pleasure you receive.
It fights the pain and misery off.

It helps you to be yourself-
  puts you socially at ease.
You say it's a choice you make.
You deny addiction and disease.

You claim you can handle it.
It doesn't affect you like everyone else.
No one knows the difference you say,
  you're still at your very best.

You justify what was wasted–
  the time and money could've been saved.
You justify you only live once
  and can carry nothing to the grave.

It's been so long that you've done it,
  you can't remember the you before.
It's a long road back to your freedom.
You must summon the strength to explore.

It's been so long that you've done it,
  you question if there was a life before.
Somehow that's how the rock works–
  convinces you you're incapable of more.

There is nothing that is good for you
  for which you must constantly lie.
There is nothing that is good for you

that will cause your dreams to die.

It's not the rock that's keeping you—
  it's the rock that's keeping you down.
It never loses sight of its goal—
  the most efficient soul taking around.

No way is that rock folding
  or just going to loosen its grip.
It ain't gonna let you go easy.
Only destruction will end this trip.

You must demand for yourself a recount.
Explore openly the established facts—
  anywhere the devil can take you,
  the Lord can lead you on back.

I hope you begin your journey soon
  to make the most of your precious life.
There's so much you can do and have in your time.
You'd know if you'd just set down the pipe.

Chapter 4

Sample Peace

1– Oh So Classy

I'm much too classy for that...
  even though I'd rather attack
  and make suffering not fiction but fact.
I could use a nail ridden bat
  to make your little brains go splat
  but I'm much too classy for that.

I'm much too classy to make you scream...
  although torturing you is a sweet dream
  and in those dreams, your blood gleams
  as it pours swimmingly out of your seams.
You should be picking your funeral theme
  but I'm much too classy I beam!

I'm much too classy to be fake...
  knowing I'd like to stab you with a rake
  or submerge you in a bottomless lake
  or ram you up the ass with a stake
  or turn you into maggot cake.

I'm much too classy for those moves to make!

I'm much too classy for this...
  to stick out my ass for you to kiss
  so I can shower you with piss.
In your navel, a wrench I want to twist,
  scar you so bad your mama would diss
  then add you to the cold case list.
Yet I'm much too classy is the gist!

I'm much too classy I can't lie...
  to have your entrails flying by
  or to construct a trophy from your eye,
  to knit a handbag from your thigh,
  to have the Lord question sadly and sigh...
  What has she done now and why?
  Why did I invent her? My My My.
  Cause with Satan she's a pretty close tie.
  Will this child ever get it right?

I could have been much too classy to write this rhyme
  but no better therapy have I been able to find.

This passion for poetic expression over time,
  has helped save me from losing my mind.
Since my pursuits are of a divine kind,
  I'd rather create than cross certain lines.

2– Following the Leader

I absolutely refuse to regress
  because in God, I have grown.
He has delivered me from more heartache
  than I ever wish to be told.
It took me a long time to realize
  it doesn't matter who felt I was worthy.
God loves you and will change you
  regardless of who thinks you deserve it.

I rediscovered my strengths
  breaking the chains of my mistakes.
I faced the realities of my past
  so my destiny I can overtake.
Perfection nor approval,
  no longer my fruitless mission.
No haters or naysayers allowed
  to impede this spiritual transition.

My candor is not aimed

at those who want just a good story.
He only allowed me to suffer
  to testify of His redeeming glory.

I won't regress, backtrack
  or be suppressed
  by the insecurities of man.
I've gotten here, this far
  because of God's unchanging hand.
I could have gotten farther
  if I had followed this close all along
  but He used my tests to build my faith
  and made something of my wrongs.

.

Don't mistake that my attitude means
  I think I'm better than most.
I just want to follow God all the time
  instead of seeking Him when I'm lost.

I won't subscribe to a doubtful mindset.
Belief is more up my alley.
Nothing will make me turn away now,
  there is no argument that is valid.

There is no more discussion.
What more do you need to ask?
Without Jesus grounded at center,
  it's just not built to last.

3– Please Reconsider

You say you feel my pain...
  when I cry all my tears.
You say you're scared of nothing
  yet you're halted by your fears.

You say you know me well,
  so completely through and through.
I can hardly tell
  since what I do is new.

You call me ever so bitter,
  frozen deep into the core.
You claim that I can't make it
  by taking this path I know!

Please reconsider how you scrutinize
  the way I choose to go.
Why do you suspiciously wonder
  when I told you long before?

My life is a promise
    made prior to my birth.
I must dedicate my soul
    to approach my life's true worth.

In everything I do and say,
    I do so with this certain will.
I await God's instructions,
    it's His plans I must fulfill.

What He has designed for me
    will be forever mine.
What I worry constantly is
    will I grasp it in time?

No wasted energy
    do I have to spend
    on devilish worries
    of a faithless friend.

We all have our own connection
    to the very same Source.
It is no fault of mine

that you tune out His voice.

Life is a journey
 that you first must begin...
Proceed with something small
 until you reach the end.

Whoever told you life was easy
 was telling the devil's lie.
It is the journey to know God
 the second we are born
 until the one we die!

4– Tragic Magic *(sexual content)*

Creep, creep go my fingers
  enjoying their slippery ride,
  probing gingerly all about
  to that luxuriously wet inside,
  seeking quite a tremendous explosion
  after a building up of the pressure.
The workings of my fingers
  elicit the orgasms that I highly treasure.

They never leave me unsatisfied
  and they don't ever play no games.
They don't demand all of my time.
Myself I don't have to change.

They've never misplaced my number
  or lost their telephone.
When all the cumming is over,
  I don't have to sleep alone.

They don't ask me for money.
They've never kept me waiting.
I never fear for my safety.
There's no arguing or endless debating.

There are no baby's mamas
  or in the closet drama.
There are no broken promises
  or disappointment over tomorrow.

My fingers will never use me
  nor ever look me in my face and lie.
They will never betray me.
My worth they will never deny.

And my fingers won't ever kick my ass
  or throw me into a wall
  and if it be that I don't succeed,
  won't be the reason that I fall.

Formerly this position
  was held down by a man
  but few seem worth the trouble

and aren't as talented as I am.

My fingers have spoiled my pussy.
It prefers its orgasms off the chart
  and I prefer their deliverer
  to not break my heart.

This awfully real celibacy
  would seem way more tragic
  if my five gifted fingers
  didn't produce so much magic.

5– Sample Peace

You can swipe a swab
  straight out of my mouth,
  ask for my urine in a cup,
  yank a hair off my scalp...
  no evidence of crack
  will you find on my person.
I'm not the first to kick
  and I won't be the last one.

I was a furious smoker.
I crushed rocks all up in my blunts,
  yet my heart desired a life still
  that my habit couldn't want.

I fell off horribly,
  my brother sadly said.
I'm the first to admit
  that I lived as if I were dead.

I understand you doubt this victory,
  I got firsthand knowledge why
  but through the grace of God
  those times have passed me by.

I'm moving forward surely
  like God's little child who could,
  so I can understand your amazement
  that from this darkness came so much good.

I won't justify my past.
I'm my own constant reminder,
  when you let go of God
  won't take Satan long to bind you.

I only speak openly
  using myself as proof.
God performed that miracle for me
  as He is waiting to do for you.

6– Can We?

Can we talk about God
  and His glory?
Can I mention His name
  without your worry?

Will it elevate or escalate
  the air that we share?
Can we disagree humanly
  yet agree that He is there?

What would you say
  to those who stray
  and those who wish to learn?
What would you be willing
  to receive and believe
  if the tables turned?

Can we talk about God

and this journey...
  particularly, yours and my story?
The ups of life and the down,
  every moment that God was found.

His certain moves that advanced your cause,
  unexpected miracles that put doubt on pause...
His truths that we know only
  because of how deeply we feel,
  even when the world tells us
  that what we feel can not be real.

Can we talk with love
  to erase the hate,
  to enjoy all the evidence
  that God is great?

That conversation is capable
  of lasting an incredible amount of long time.
Even a smidgen of His goodness
  will intensely blow your mind.

So may we commence

with the Godly discussions?
As long as we're alive,
we can still learn something.

7- The Waiting Room

Patience is my hardest part of faith.
I wait now to see the way
  the Lord will lead me in His time.

My life seems suspended.
I call on Him helplessly.
I wait restlessly
  for the Lord to interject
  something unknown and unexpected
  to reinforce once again,
  I can not exist without His blessings.

I endured many painful experiences
  because of my unwillingness to obey God-
  to see what I wanted to see
  instead of what really was.

Life is a moment to moment journey
  so I learn to follow Him more carefully.

I contemplate that very second
  I should step out in pursuit of my destiny.

But how does patience relate to faith?

Sometimes I wait and I watch
  curiously,
  as others go by
  taking their fate,
  enjoying their life.

Sometimes I wait and I watch
  anxiously,
  as others go by
  moving too fast,
  they fall short and die.

Am I receiving His signal clear–
  is now my chief source of debating.
Don't want to be caught pushing ahead,
  when I should be patiently waiting.

Then again,

I don't want to be standing there
when the Lord is cheering I go.
With some things to know you got them right,
it takes a lifetime to know for sure.

8– You Got Me… Somewhere *(sexual content)*

When you come near me,
  my nipples still get hard.
My stomach still gets queasy
  and my clit sounds the same alarm.

Sometimes I get dizzy
  trying to hold my passion so tight.
For somehow in your presence,
  my defenses lose their fight.

My mind is now questioning
  how such a tremendous desire
  has survived all this fury
  that your actions have inspired.
Yet, if I said I still didn't want you,
  I'd surely be a liar.
And from battling all these emotions,
  surely am I tired.

I'm scared of you now,
  even more than before
  because somehow you've penetrated
  my hidden and invisible doors
  and even when it hurts,
  it is you whom l adore.

You got me somewhere…
  between forgiveness and forgetting,
  a ride from this hell
  straight back to our heaven.

U got me somewhere…
  a place I hardly go,
  a place that is foreign
  but one I'd like to know.

How can I let you back next to me,
  when still I sense so much danger?
Full speed screams my heart
  as caution becomes a stranger.

You got me somewhere…

contemplating...
all that I may lose
and since the day we found each other,
all I fear losing is you.

Forgiveness demands a change in my ways
in how I react to anger.
Every little disagreement
doesn't put my soul in danger.

You've got me somewhere....
for a while,
I sense you've been waiting.

You know you're all I want,
so why am I still debating?

9– The Party Planner

You make a girl feel mighty welcome
  here on this planet Earth.
You roll out Your loving carpet for everyone
  but most don't know their true worth.

I had no idea of mine.
At one time I was clueless,
  downright depressed inside,
  feeling unloved, abandoned and useless.

On my most wanting and faithless days,
  mine own agenda I impatiently pursued.
Now my life is so much better
  since I left all the planning up to You.

Mighty welcome I want You to feel here,
  I can hear You, my Savior say.
Learn to hear and distinguish my voice.
They are called Commandments

because they are not a choice.

Your plan is all laid out...
  a glorious green and blue spread.
The amenities include fresh air and water,
  bountiful herbs, plants, and grains for bread.

You're being born into a family,
  forever yours but never perfect.
You'll have friends and adventures,
  many opportunities and a package to work it.

And when you follow faithfully
  your planted dreams and hopes,
  you'll discover there's more to this world
  that in this lifetime, you will ever know.

That's the kind of life
  possible to all by my Savior.
Following Him isn't always easy
  but it sure has the best flavor.

Alphabetical Index

Topical Index

Most of my work is definitely for mature audiences. Here is a quick reference guide of other relevant categories:

Family Friendly

(These pieces can be shared with the entire family and there shouldn't be any awkward moments.)

Drugs and Recovery

(If you are in a place of addiction or love someone who is, these pieces may provide some insight.)

Naughty
(Do not let your kids read this stuff unless awkward moments are your thing.)

Made in the USA
Middletown, DE
02 August 2015